EGYPT 2013 INTERNATIONAL RELIGIOUS FREEDOM REPORT

Executive Summary

Respect for religious freedom remained poor during the year under both former President Mohamed Morsy's administration and the current interim government. On July 3, Mohamed Morsy was removed and Adly Mansour was named interim president. The 2012 constitution, in effect until its suspension on July 3, stipulated "freedom of belief is an inviolable right," but only guaranteed the freedom to perform religious rituals for adherents of Islam, Christianity, and Judaism. Interim President Adly Mansour issued a Constitutional Declaration on July 8 that superseded the 2012 constitution. The declaration guarantees freedom of religion only for adherents of Islam, Christianity, and Judaism. Both the 2012 constitution and the Constitutional Declaration declare Islam is the official religion of the state and the principles of sharia (Islamic law) are the primary sources of legislation. Certain laws and government policies and practices further limit constitutional guarantees of religious freedom. Defaming Islam, Christianity, or Judaism is prohibited by law. As required by law, prosecutors investigated dozens of criminal complaints filed by citizens against those whose statements or actions were alleged to be blasphemous, denigrating of religion, or insulting to the Prophet Muhammed or other historical religious figures. In contrast to previous years, some of these cases were prosecuted, leading to the conviction of at least nine people during the year. Non-Muslims must obtain a presidential decree to build new places of worship. While recognized and unrecognized religious minorities mostly worshiped without harassment, the government generally failed to prevent, investigate, or prosecute crimes against members of religious minority groups, which fostered a climate of impunity. The government arrested, detained, or harassed members of minority Muslim groups. The Morsy administration routinely failed to condemn incendiary speech, including anti-Semitic and anti-Christian speech in mosque sermons and during broadcasts by Islamic "televangelists." The interim government undertook serious measures to stop incendiary speech in mosques and on Islamist television channels. In some respects, such as in the number of permits granted for the construction of churches, there were indications of slight improvements in government practices under the interim government.

There were reports of societal abuses and discrimination based on religious affiliation, belief, or practice. Lethal sectarian attacks increased during the year. Islamist-led mobs carried out acts of violence, intimidation, compelled expulsions, and collective punishment against Christians, especially in Upper Egypt (the southern part of the country). Non-governmental organizations (NGOs) reported assailants attacked at least 42 churches between August 14 and August 17 in various governorates, resulting in the looting and destruction of at least 37 churches and the deaths of at least six Christians who were targeted because of their religious identity. Christians, Shia, Bahais, and other minorities faced personal and collective discrimination, especially in government employment and in their ability to build, renovate, and repair places of worship.

The U.S. President, Secretary of State, Ambassador, and other senior administration officials emphasized in public and private statements the government's responsibility to protect the rights of all citizens, regardless of religion. All raised strong concerns about religious violence and discrimination with senior government officials and directly with the public. In August the President condemned sectarian violence in Egypt, including attacks on churches. In a March visit to Cairo, the Secretary of State Kerry emphasized the importance of ensuring freedom of religion for all Egyptians, regardless of their faith, with equal rights and protections under the law. In November in Cairo, Secretary Kerry condemned attacks on churches and worshipers and urged Foreign Minister Nabil Fahmy to hold perpetrators of such violence accountable. The Ambassador met with senior religious leaders to discuss ways to reduce sectarian tensions and discrimination. In May the Ambassador released a statement reaffirming the U.S. position that freedom of religion is a universal right and encouraging the government to make improving the state of religious freedom a top priority. In April the Ambassador raised religious freedom in meetings with the Prime Minister and the Minister of Justice. The U.S. government continued to sponsor programs to promote religious tolerance and freedom.

Section I. Religious Demography

The U.S. government estimates the population at 85.3 million (July 2013 estimate). Approximately 90 percent of the population is Sunni Muslim and about 10 percent is Christian. The majority of Christians belong to the Coptic Orthodox Church. Other Christian communities together constitute less than 2 percent of the population and include the Armenian Apostolic, Catholic (Armenian, Chaldean, Greek, Melkite, Roman, and Syrian), Maronite, Orthodox (Greek and Syrian), and Anglican/Episcopalian churches, which range in size from several thousand to hundreds of thousands. A Protestant community, established in the mid-19th century, includes the following churches: Presbyterian, Baptist, Brethren, Open Brethren, Revival of Holiness (Nahdat al-Qadaasa), Faith (Al-Eyman), Church of God, Christian Model Church (Al-Mithaal Al-Masihi), Apostolic, Grace (An-

EGYPT

Ni'ma), Pentecostal, Apostolic Grace, Church of Christ, Gospel Missionary (Al-Kiraaza bil Ingil), and the Message Church of Holland (Ar-Risaala). There are also followers of the Seventh-day Adventist Church.

Shia Muslims constitute less than 1 percent of the population. There are also small groups of Quranists and Ahmadi Muslims. The country's Jewish community numbers fewer than 100 persons, many of them senior citizens. There are 1,000 to 1,500 Jehovah's Witnesses and about 2,000 Bahais.

Christians reside throughout the country, although the percentage of Christians is higher in Upper Egypt and in some sections of Cairo and Alexandria.

Many foreign religious groups, including Roman Catholics and Protestants, have been present in the country for more than a century. These groups are engaged in education, social, and development work. Some foreigners are members of The Church of Jesus Christ of Latter-day Saints (Mormons), a group the government does not recognize but allows to meet in private residences.

Section II. Status of Government Respect for Religious Freedom

Legal/Policy Framework

The 2012 constitution, in effect until July 3, provided for some freedom of religion, but certain provisions limited that freedom in practice. The Constitutional Declaration issued by interim President Adly Mansour on July 8, which superseded the 2012 constitution, retained guarantees for freedom of religion only for adherents of Islam, Christianity, and Judaism, excluding adherents of other religions. Other laws and government policies limit religious freedom.

The suspended 2012 constitution stated "freedom of belief is an inviolable right" but required the government to guarantee the freedom to practice religious rites and establish places of worship only to adherents of Islam, Christianity, and Judaism. The constitution stipulated these rights were limited "as regulated by law." It also stated the canonical principles of Christians and Jews were the main source of legislation for their personal status laws, religious affairs, and the selection of their spiritual leaders. By implication, followers of other religious groups, including Bahais and Christian churches the government did not recognize, were precluded from applying their own religious laws and restricted from building places of worship. The 2012 constitution guaranteed the freedom to establish

EGYPT

places of worship for the "three Abrahamic faiths" – Islam, Christianity, and Judaism – if done "in accordance with the law."

The 2012 constitution specified Islam as the state religion and the principles of sharia as the primary source of legislation. It broadly defined the principles of sharia to encompass all attestations and precepts found within Sunni schools of Islamic jurisprudence and stated the opinion of Al Azhar University's Senior Scholars Committee "shall be taken on matters pertaining to Islamic sharia." Secularists and Christians in particular later criticized these provisions for being overly vague, leaving room for future interpretation that could be either benign or harmful to religious freedom, depending on the views of those leading the government or Al Azhar.

The 2012 constitution prohibited offending or criticizing prophets and messengers, and the penal code sets out the associated criminal penalties, including a minimum of six months and a maximum of five years' imprisonment for citizens who promulgate "extremist thoughts with the aim of inciting strife, demeaning or defaming any of the heavenly religions, or inflicting damage to the national unity."

The Constitutional Declaration of July 8 limits freedom of belief and the practice of religious rites to adherents of Islam, Christianity, and Judaism. Like the 2012 constitution, it declares Islam the official religion of the state and the principles of sharia the primary sources of legislation. Unlike the 2012 constitution, which stated "freedom of belief is an inviolable right," the Constitutional Declaration does not include a reference to any broader right to freedom of religion. It defines the principles of sharia as including "evidences and jurisprudence rules and established sources in the Sunni canons," a narrower definition than the 2012 constitution. Unlike the 2012 constitution, it makes no mention of the role of Al Azhar University's Senior Scholars Committee in matters pertaining to sharia. The declaration contains none of the 2012 constitution's provisions permitting Christians and Jews to refer to their religious laws in matters pertaining to personal status issues, religious practices, and the selection of their spiritual leaders.

The Supreme Council of the Armed Forces (SCAF) issued a decree in 2011 to amend provisions of the penal code to explicitly prohibit religious and other forms of discrimination but did not include enforcement mechanisms. Discrimination in government and private hiring remains widespread.

EGYPT

Although religious conversions are not prohibited by law, local officials generally act in accordance with sharia, which forbids Muslims from converting to another religion, and refuse to recognize conversions on legal documents.

Neither the Constitutional Declaration nor the civil or penal code prohibits proselytizing; however, the government imposes legal penalties on activities related to proselytizing by non-Muslims, including "disrupting social cohesion." The government generally tolerates foreign religious workers on the condition they do not proselytize among Muslims. Non-Muslim minorities and foreign religious workers generally refrain from proselytizing to avoid legal penalties and extra-legal repercussions from authorities and local Islamists.

The 2012 constitution guaranteed that principles of the canonical laws of Jews and Christians form the basis of legislation governing their personal affairs. However in marital affairs, the law still stipulates that spouses must be members of the same religious denomination for courts to apply these canonical laws. When spouses are members of differing religious denominations, the courts apply sharia. Despite the 2012 constitutional guarantee that personal status laws would be adjudicated on the basis of the canonical principles of the three Abrahamic faiths, all Egyptians remained subject to sharia in matters of inheritance.

In family law, the government only recognizes the religious legal principles of Islam, Christianity, and Judaism. Cases involving individuals who do not adhere to these three faiths are adjudicated based on civil law. The government recognizes only the marriages of Christians, Jews, and Muslims. Non-Muslim men must convert to Islam to marry Muslim women, although non-Muslim women need not convert to marry Muslim men. A non-Muslim woman who converts to Islam, however, must divorce her husband if he is not Muslim and is unwilling to convert. Custody of children is then awarded to the mother.

Sharia prevents Coptic men and Muslim women from marrying each other and does not legally recognize a marriage outside the country between such individuals. Coptic Orthodox laws prohibit all mixed marriages; however, in situations where these laws conflict with sharia, sharia takes precedence. Although the Coptic Church prohibits all mixed marriages, the government recognizes marriages between Christian women and Muslim men. The law provides for "khul" (divorce), which allows a Muslim woman to obtain a divorce without her husband's consent provided that she is willing to forgo all of her financial rights, including alimony, dowry, and other benefits.

EGYPT

The minor children of Muslim converts to Christianity, and in some cases adult children who were minors when their parents converted, automatically remain classified as Muslims because the government does not recognize conversion from Islam. This is true irrespective of the religion of the other parent.

The Ministry of Education bans the hijab (Islamic headscarf) in primary schools, but allows it in preparatory and secondary schools upon written request from a girl's parent.

In public schools Muslim students are required to take courses on "principles of Islam" and Christian students are required to take courses on "principles of Christianity" in all grades. Students who are neither Muslim nor Christian must choose one or the other course; they may not opt out or change from one to the other.

Various ministries may obtain court orders to ban or confiscate books and works of art. The Council of Ministers may ban works it deems offensive to public morals, detrimental to religion, or likely to cause a breach of the peace. The Islamic Research Center of Al Azhar has the legal authority to censor and confiscate any publications dealing with the Quran and the authoritative Islamic traditions (Hadith), and to confiscate publications, tapes, speeches, and artistic materials deemed inconsistent with Islamic law.

The Ministry of Islamic Endowments (Awqaf) is required to license all mosques; however, many operate without licenses. The government has the authority to appoint and monitor the imams who lead prayers in licensed mosques and pays for their salaries. In practice, government control over mosques decreased after the 2011 revolution, but strengthened following the removal of former President Mohamed Morsy in July. A September decree by the ministry prevents imams who are not graduates of Al Azhar from preaching in licensed and unlicensed mosques. The decree prohibits holding Friday prayers in mosques smaller than 80 square meters, bans unlicensed mosques from holding Friday congregational prayer services, and requires Friday sermons to follow government "talking points." Local media reported the ministry did in fact stop some non-Azharite preachers from delivering sermons in mosques later in the year. The government does not compensate Christian clergy.

Non-Muslims must obtain a presidential decree to build new places of worship, but can undertake basic repairs and maintenance with written notification to local authorities. A Ministry of Interior (MOI) decree issued in the 1930s and still generally followed specifies a set of 10 conditions the government must consider, including that a church may be no closer than 100 meters (340 feet) from an existing mosque and churches in Muslim-majority neighborhoods need local approval before forwarding an application to the president for a decree for construction of a new church. In 2005, then-President Mubarak delegated the authority to permit Christian denominations to expand or rebuild existing churches to the country's 26 governors. Governors must examine all applications and their supporting documentation within 30 days.

To obtain official recognition, a religious group must submit a request to the MOI's Religious Affairs Department. The department then determines whether the group would, in its view, pose a threat or upset national unity or social peace. As part of this determination, the department consults leading religious institutions, including the Coptic Orthodox Church and Al Azhar. The registration is then referred to the president for decision. If a religious group fails to obtain official registration, its members potentially face detention and prosecution for harming social cohesion or, under article 98(f) of the Penal Code, for denigrating religions.

The Penal Code, including article 98(f), lists a range of loosely defined actions constituting the crime of denigration of religions. These actions include "promoting extreme ideas with the purpose of stirring strife, despising or denigrating one of the heavenly religions or a sect included in them, or harming national unity."

Only Islam, Christianity, or Judaism may be indicated in the religion field of government-issued national identity cards. Muslim-born citizens who convert from Islam may not change that field. Members of the Bahai community are able to obtain identity cards with a "dash" in the religion field, but their marriages are not recognized or listed on the identity cards. Since 2011 Christians who convert to Islam and then back to Christianity may amend their national identification cards to reflect their chosen faith. Hundreds of Muslims officially reconverted to Christianity during the year.

The law does not recognize the Bahai Faith and bans Bahai institutions and community activities. Bahais are able, however, to worship privately and engage in celebrations such as the Bahai New Year. The lack of formal recognition for the Bahai Faith is an obstacle to registering marriages and processing inheritance. Although Muslims and Christians follow sharia or their respective church laws for personal status issues, including marriage, the state does not recognize Bahai religious law, and there is no recourse to civil law for personal status issues. Since the state refuses to issue national identity cards recognizing Bahai marriage, married Bahais are denied the basic legal rights of married couples and also face difficulties in banking, real estate, business, and other joint legal transactions. Additionally, an Egyptian-born Bahai cannot sponsor a foreign-born spouse's permanent residency.

The quasi-governmental National Council for Human Rights is charged with strengthening protections, raising awareness, and ensuring the observance of human rights and fundamental freedoms, including religious freedom. It is also charged with monitoring enforcement and application of international agreements. Interim government leaders insist the Council will play a watchdog role in monitoring violations of civil liberties. The Council claims to have undertaken a fact-finding mission into the attacks on places of worship since June 30, but did not issue any findings by year's end. On December 21, interim President Mansour issued a decree forming an independent fact-finding committee into the violent events that followed the June 30 demonstrations. The committee is directed to present its final report and recommendations to the president within six months.

Government Practices

The government failed to protect Christians and their property effectively when they were attacked in instances of sectarian violence throughout the country. The government continued to harass Shia and prohibit conversion from Islam. While recognized and unrecognized religious minorities mostly worshiped without harassment, the government generally failed to prevent, investigate, or prosecute crimes targeting members of religious minority groups, which fostered a climate of impunity. The government routinely failed to investigate and prosecute crimes against Christians and other religious minorities.

As required by law, prosecutors investigated dozens of criminal complaints filed by citizens against individuals whose statements or actions were alleged to be blasphemous, denigrating of religion, or insulting to the Prophet Muhammed and other historical religious figures. Some of these cases went to trials, resulting in the convictions of nine people, a departure from Mubarak-era practice whereby such cases were rarely prosecuted. Courts convicted four Muslims and five Christians, including two children under the age of 11, of denigrating religion. Most of these cases were filed against individuals in Upper Egypt, according to the Egyptian Initiative for Personal Rights (EIPR), a human rights NGO. EIPR reported most of these cases targeted regular citizens rather than public figures, a departure from the past two decades. For example, in June the Luxor

EGYPT

Misdemeanor Court fined elementary teacher Damiana Abdel Nour, a 23-year-old Copt, EGP 100,000 ($14,400) for denigrating Islam and evangelizing among her students. Three of her students' parents had filed a complaint against her, accusing her of denigrating Islam and evangelizing among her students during a class on religious life in ancient Egypt. According to EIPR, 10 of her 13 students denied that she had committed either offense. Abdel Nour's request to appeal the verdict was granted and court proceedings were ongoing at year's end.

In June the Beba Court of Beni Suef similarly sentenced author Karam Saber, a Muslim, to five years in prison and an EGP 1,000 ($144) fine for denigrating religions in his book *Where is God?*, which was released in 2011. The prosecution consulted a church in Beni Suef and Al Azhar for their opinion on the book. Both institutions denounced the book saying it contradicted "divine religions" and damaged Egyptian societal values. Eight local NGOs criticized Saber's trial and conviction, including the prosecution's reliance on claims by private citizens irrespective of available evidence, the court's reliance on the opinions of religious organizations to assess literary works, and the impact such convictions had on the freedom of opinion and expression. Saber's request to appeal the verdict was granted and slated for reconsideration in early 2014.

Authorities arrested Coptic activist Alber Saber Ayad in Cairo in September 2012 for posting an inflammatory and anti-Islamic amateur video on a social media platform and for previous online blog entries that were critical of religion. In December 2012, the Marg Misdemeanor Court sentenced Ayad to three years in prison and a fine of EGP 1,000 ($144) after finding him guilty of defaming Islam. After posting bail, he was released on December 17, 2012, and left the country. Ayad appealed the verdict and his appeal was rejected in January 2013. He remained a fugitive at year's end.

The Nasr City Misdemeanor Court sentenced Salafist televangelist Sheikh Ahmed Abdullah, also known as Sheikh Abu Islam, to 11 years' imprisonment with labor for denigrating Christianity, inciting strife, and disturbing public security. Abu Islam had encouraged a child to urinate on a Bible before tearing and burning it during protests in front of the U.S. embassy in Cairo in September 2012. Upon appeal, the sentence was later reduced to five years' imprisonment. He was also sentenced to another three years in prison and an EGP 10,000 ($1,440) fine for denigrating Christianity in statements he made on a television program. Abu Islam also appealed the second verdict and his case was adjourned until February 2014.

EGYPT

In April police arrested three family members of a young Coptic man in Al Wasta, Beni Suef, who reportedly married a 21-year-old woman who had converted from Islam to Christianity and then fled the country with her. The man's elderly parents and cousin were detained on charges of assisting the conversion of the woman to Christianity and coercing her to denigrate Islam. The Prosecutor General ordered their release in early December.

Courts sometimes sentenced Christians to prison terms that exceeded those given to Muslims convicted of the same crimes. In April 2012, a dispute over a speed bump outside the Abu Qurqas residence of Alaa Reda Roshdy, a local Christian politician, led to confrontations between Muslims and Christians resulting in two deaths, at least four injuries, and property damage to a number of Coptic residences and properties. In May 2012, the exceptional Higher State Security Court sentenced each of the 12 Copts involved in the incident to life in prison after finding two of them guilty of premeditated murder and the others guilty of rioting, destruction of property and/or possessing weapons, crimes that ordinarily carry maximum penalties of a few years in prison. The court acquitted all eight Muslim suspects. Then-Prime Minister Hesham Kandil accepted a petition by the Christian defendants' lawyers, requesting a retrial in December 2012. In the retrial, which concluded in July, the life prison sentences for the 12 Christians were affirmed. The Muslim defendants, however, were each sentenced to 15 years in prison for theft, rioting, and destruction of property. An EIPR statement criticized the court proceedings and verdict, stating the Christian defendants' lawyers had not been allowed for a second time to present their defenses to the court. Some of the sentences were given in absentia.

In November 2012, the Cairo Criminal Court sentenced in absentia seven Christians to death for their alleged connection to the production of an inflammatory and anti-Islamic amateur video. An eighth suspect, a U.S. citizen, was sentenced in absentia to five years in prison for the misdemeanor crime of demeaning religion. According to local media, the prosecution claimed the suspects used religion to spread extremist ideas with the aim of inciting sectarianism and defaming one of the heavenly religions, and damaging national unity and societal peace. The grand mufti ratified the death sentences in January in a non-binding opinion. All those sentenced are reportedly living outside the country.

The government did not investigate and prosecute any military or police commanders reportedly responsible for ordering or failing to prevent violence against the mostly Coptic demonstrators at the Maspiro radio and television building in Cairo in October 2011 in which 25 persons were killed and over 300 were injured. In September 2012, a military court sentenced three low-ranking soldiers to between two and three years in prison for their involvement in the incident. Two Copts accused of stealing weapons during the Maspiro incident were sentenced to three years in prison in February. One of the Copts was granted an appeal. The retrial commenced in December.

The government continued to sponsor "customary reconciliation sessions" after sectarian attacks and inter-communal violence instead of prosecuting the perpetrators of the crimes. These extrajudicial sessions were usually attended by governorate officials or the Ministry of Interior, along with Christian and Muslim clergymen who represented the conflicting parties. In these sessions, the parties agree to a number of measures to stop the conflict, which may include punishment of the perpetrators by expulsion from the village, compensation for the affected parties, or a penalty clause for the future breaching of any agreement. In most cases, the parties also agree to drop all formal charges and lawsuits. Christians routinely viewed the decisions emanating from these sessions as largely unfair, but were subject to political pressure to participate. In December, following a customary reconciliation session in Minya, the governorate's Coptic Orthodox Bishop Makarious − in a break from past Church policy − declared the Church no longer would acknowledge reconciliation sessions because they effectively undermined the rule of law and represented a temporary solution to a protracted sectarian problem.

In August the government sponsored reconciliation sessions following sectarian clashes in the village of East Beni Ahmed, which left one Muslim dead, 18 injured, and several Christian-owned houses and businesses looted and destroyed. The clashes reportedly erupted following an argument between a Copt and a Muslim at a cafe in East Beni Ahmed over a pro-army song. Several suspects were arrested and detained pending investigations for murder, attempted murder for the purpose of terrorizing, thuggery, and the possession of unlicensed firearms and ammunition. A week later, the secretary-general of the governorate, members of the Islamist group Al Gamaa Al Islamiya, security officials, and Christian clerics held a widely-publicized reconciliation session. Participants in the session agreed all legal suits filed in relation to the incidents would be dropped and anyone engaging in inciting violence in the future would be expelled from the village. Contrary to the expectations of the Christians in the community, participants did not agree to compensate those affected by the violence. The Coptic Orthodox Church estimated damage to Christian property at roughly EGP 3.4 million ($489,350). The participants also agreed to create an "arbitration committee" to resolve future sectarian conflicts at their inception. Following the reconciliation, 30 claimants dropped cases they had filed against a number of arrested suspects. Similar sessions took place following sectarian violence in the governorate of Beni Suef.

The government failed to pass a law eliminating the discriminatory permit process by which Christians build and repair places of worship. The government promised to consider such a law after both the Imbaba riots in May 2011 and the Maspiro violence in October 2011. The Coptic Orthodox Church and Al Azhar, along with some Protestant churches, reportedly agreed on draft legislation in late October 2011, but the government took no action. During his tenure as president, Mohamed Morsy issued only one decree authorizing the construction of one "apartment-sized" church intended to serve a community of 1,000 Coptic families. Interim government President Mansour issued decrees licensing the construction of three churches, two in August and a third in October. According to church leadership, the building requests for these churches were submitted several years earlier.

In April six Copts and a Muslim died and 22 people were injured in sectarian clashes in Al Khosous, Qalioubiya. During the Christian victims' funeral, held at St. Mark's Coptic Orthodox Cathedral in the heart of Cairo and attended by thousands of Copts, clashes erupted among mourners, police, and residents near the cathedral, leaving a Copt and a Muslim dead and 89 injured. According to the Ministry of Interior, 16 police officers were also injured. According to EIPR, security forces fired teargas canisters excessively at mourners in front of the cathedral's gate and deep into the cathedral. Video recordings of the incidents showed police failing to stop assailants from throwing rocks and bottles at the cathedral despite being in plain sight and having armored vehicles nearby. On April 8, then-President Morsy ordered an immediate investigation into the incidents and public announcement of the results. He stated the law would be applied with firmness to the perpetrators. The public prosecutor opened investigations on 21 suspects for rioting, possession of bladed weapons and firearms, and jeopardizing national unity and communal peace. At year's end, the investigations were ongoing.

There have been no reports of violent anti-Semitic incidents in recent years; however, anti-Semitic sentiments routinely appeared in both government-owned and private media, and the government made few public attempts to distinguish between anti-Semitism and opposition to Israeli policies and practices. In January satirist Bassem Youssef broadcast video clips from 2010 showing then-President

EGYPT

Morsy delivering a speech urging Egyptians to "nurse our children and our grandchildren on hatred" for Jews and Zionists. Later in January Morsy told members of a U.S. congressional delegation his remarks had been taken out of context. He also asserted his respect for all religious creeds, saying he drew a distinction between followers of Judaism and Israelis, who he said persistently mistreated Palestinians in the occupied territories. In May then-President Morsy appointed Alaa Abdel-Aziz Minister of Culture. Abdel-Aziz had previously provided input on several chapters of the anti-Semitic "Encyclopedia of Jews, Judaism, and Zionism."

For the third consecutive year, authorities cancelled the Abu Hassira celebrations scheduled for January, preventing the annual pilgrimage by non-Egyptian Jews, mostly Israelis, to the shrine of 19th-century scholar Rabbi Yaakov Abu Hassira. The government cited security concerns in justifying its decision.

Government and official Islamic institutions used anti-Shia rhetoric. In June then-President Morsy attended a conference organized by Islamist figures and sheikhs dubbed "For the Victory of Syria." During the conference held in Cairo Stadium and aired live on state-owned television, Salafi preacher Sheikh Mohamed Al Arifi described Shia as "non-believers who must be killed," according to a report by Human Rights Watch (HRW).

In November the Ministry of Awqaf instructed imams to prohibit Shia commemorations of Ashura (a solemn religious occasion for Shias, commemorating the martyrdom of Hussein ibn Ali, the grandson of Prophet Muhammed) in mosques. Minister of Awqaf Mohamed Mokhtar Gomaa also called on the Ministry of Interior to prevent such celebrations. Sheikh Usama Al Hadidi, the imam of Al Hussein Mosque (named after Hussein ibn Ali), said he had received instructions from the Ministry of Awqaf to prevent Shia rituals in the mosque and confirmed that none took place. According to members of the Shia community, Shia leaders received threats from Salafis not to hold celebrations, which prompted them not to hold any to avoid potential violence. Amr Abdullah, a Shia activist, was arrested during Ashura outside Al Hussein Mosque following altercations with a group of Salafis. Salafi groups had reportedly been in the vicinity of the mosque to "monitor the Shia presence," according to EIPR. Abdullah remained in detention at year's end on charges of denigrating Islam.

Government entities continued to discriminate against Christians in hiring. Christians continued to be under-represented relative to their population in senior government leadership positions, both elected and appointed. Three Christians

EGYPT

were elected and 12 appointed to the Shura Council, the acting legislative body during the first half of the year, amounting to fewer than 6 percent of the seats but an improvement over two percent in the Shura Council of 2010. Political parties nominated relatively few Christians to run in elections as candidates. The cabinet headed by former Prime Minister Hesham Kandil included one Christian cabinet minister out of a total of 35. There were few Christians in the upper ranks of the security services and armed forces. The 50-member Constitution Amending Committee, which amended the 2012 constitution from September through December, included four Christian representatives, three of whom were representatives of the Orthodox, Catholic, and Protestant Churches of Egypt.

The government discriminated against religious minorities in public sector hiring and staff appointments to public universities. There were no Christians serving as presidents or deans of the country's 17 public universities. Of nearly 700 president, dean, or vice dean positions in the country's public university system, Christians rarely filled more than one or two. Only Muslims could study at Al Azhar University, a publicly funded institution with approximately half a million students. Additionally, the government barred non-Muslims from employment in public university training programs for Arabic language teachers because the curriculum involves study of the Quran.

Following the attacks on a large number of churches after the dispersal of the Islamist sit-ins of Raba'a El Adawiya and Al Nahda Squares in Cairo on August 14, Defense Minister General Abdel Fattah Al Sisi announced the army would rebuild destroyed churches at the expense of the armed forces. In December Coptic Orthodox Bishop Makarious of Minya told local media the rebuilding process had commenced. The Bishop stated the engineering corps of the armed forces had started to rebuild Prince Tadros Shatbi Church in downtown Minya, in addition to a Christian school, as part of the first stage of the restoration effort, which included five churches and a school in four different cities in the governorate of Minya. The restoration process also reportedly began in the governorates of Beni Suef, Fayoum, Sohag, and Assiut. The Orthodox Church estimated the cost of restoring the damaged churches and schools nationwide to be approximately 188 million EGP ($27 million). The armed forces also donated 250,000 EGP ($36,000) for re-stocking 32 mostly Christian-owned pharmacies affected by the attacks.

The representation of Copts in the cabinet improved in the interim government, which had three Christian ministers in a cabinet of 36 ministers, including the

EGYPT

important post of Minister of Industry and Trade, versus only one during the Morsy administration.

Government Inaction

The government often failed to prevent societal violence and assaults against Christians and their property despite repeatedly stressing it was committed to protecting national unity and confronting sectarian violence.

On April 5, clashes erupted between Christians and Muslims in the city of Al Khosous in the governorate of Qalioubiya after residents purportedly mistook swastikas drawn by children on the wall of an Azharite institute for crosses. During the clashes, a Copt reportedly shot randomly at people in the streets, killing one Muslim and injuring three others. Violence escalated after the imam of a nearby mosque called Muslims to confront the Christians, according to a report on the incident prepared by the quasi-governmental National Council for Human Rights. Three houses and three businesses owned by Christians were looted and torched. The Al Khosous Baptist Church was attacked with Molotov cocktails that scorched its facade. A squad of 10 police officers was dispatched to the scene two hours later but was unable to quell the violence. Unknown assailants then opened fire at dozens of Copts who had gathered in front of St. George Coptic Orthodox Church, killing four Christians. According to eyewitness accounts reported by EIPR, police threw tear-gas canisters inside the church before leaving the area without halting the attack. Two other Christians were later killed in the area. The authorities tried 43 defendants in relation to the incident, including for the killing of the Muslim victim, the attempted killings of three others, possession of weapons, and arson. The prosecution did not present any suspects for the killings of the Christian victims. On December 14, the Banha Criminal Court sentenced Hany Farouk Awad, a Christian, to life imprisonment with labor for the killing of the Muslim victim. For the other charges, the Court sentenced each of two Christians to 15 years in prison and eight Muslims to sentences between six months and five years in prison. The remaining 32 defendants, all Muslim, were acquitted, according to an activist lawyer. Christian activists attributed the outcome to inadequate investigations by the prosecution.

On June 23, a mob of thousands of angry villagers led by Salafist sheikhs killed four Shia citizens in the village of Zawyat Abu Muslam in Giza. The attack came after weeks of hateful speech by Salafist preachers in the village against Shia, according to the Arab Network for Human Rights Information. Among the four victims was 66-year-old Hassan Shehata, a prominent Shia figure. According to the Ministry of Interior, Shehata was preaching to 34 Shia when the attack occurred. Locals were reportedly provoked by the Shia rituals taking place in their village. A mob of villagers besieged the house where the rituals were allegedly taking place, threw stones and Molotov cocktails at it, and dragged four individuals into the street where they were beaten with large sticks and stones, according to the South Giza Prosecution based on preliminary examination of the bodies. Police officers did nothing to stop the attack, arriving late to the scene according to eyewitnesses. Then-President Mohamed Morsy and Prime Minister Hisham Kandil issued statements condemning the violence but failed to address the right to religious freedom for Shia, according to HRW. Authorities initiated an investigation into seven individuals suspected of murder, attempted murder, arson, vandalism, resisting authorities, and thuggery in relation to the incident. The investigations were ongoing at year's end.

On July 5, a crowd of Muslims beat and stabbed Sobhi Magdi Eskander, a Christian accused of killing a Muslim by family members of the deceased in Al Dabaiya village in Luxor. Security forces responding to Eskander's request for help told the crowd that he had been killed. After police left the area, several hundred local Muslims attempted to storm Christian homes. Police officers later returned, but were unable to control the growing crowd. Mobs attacked Christian homes over the course of two days, leaving four Copts killed, six injured, and 21 houses looted and vandalized, some of which were completely destroyed or burned to the ground. According to EIPR, police refused to evacuate male Christians during the attacks, allowing only Christian women into an armored vehicle departing the area.

On August 7, 16 non-governmental and civil society organizations issued a joint statement in which they denounced the negligence of state institutions for failing to provide the necessary protection to Christians, decisively confront sectarian attacks, and enforce the law by arresting those responsible. This negligence, the statement said, "revealed that the pattern of impunity which spread during the Mubarak era and remained in place through the rule of the Muslim Brotherhood continues to this day, even after both regimes were overthrown."

In October five Christians − including two children − and a young Muslim man were killed after unknown assailants opened fire on Copts waiting outside St. Mary's Church in Al-Warraq, Giza, where a wedding was about to commence. According to the church's leaders and witnesses, there were no security forces present at the time of the attack. They also confirmed security officers had been absent from their regular positions outside the church since the August 14 attacks on churches, which followed the security services' dispersal on the day of the pro-Morsy sit-ins in Cairo and Giza.

The government failed to protect Christians in the village of Delga in the township of Deir Mawas in Minya during a complete security vacuum in the village that lasted over a month. The violence in Delga reportedly started in late June, shortly before the removal of former President Morsy. After authorities dispersed pro-Morsy sit-ins in Cairo and Giza on August 14, security forces withdrew from Delga after local Islamists attacked police stations there and around the country, leaving the village without any police presence until September 15, when army and police forces were able to reassert control. Before the return of security forces, many Christian residents of Delga left their homes only when absolutely necessary out of fear of being accosted by armed Muslims or opportunistic young men who extorted "taxes" from them, according to media reports and phone interviews with eyewitnesses. According to local residents, kidnappers targeted Delga's Christians, demanding and receiving ransoms of between EGP 100,000 and 150,000 ($14,400 to 21,600). Some Christian families reportedly fled the village out of fear of attacks.

In general, reports of kidnappings increased throughout the country after January 2011. In population centers, wealthy Christians and Muslims alike were victimized. In Upper Egypt, however, Christians bore the brunt of these crimes. According to media reports, interviews with Coptic activist attorneys, and Coptic clergy, Christians in Minya Governorate were specifically targeted by criminals for kidnappings for ransom throughout the year. Christians were targeted reportedly because they were perceived to have better access to ransom sums and to lack the communal strength in rural areas to seek political or legal recourse. The September abduction of Hany Sedhom in the town of Naga Hamadi, Minya Governorate, attracted local and international attention. Sedhom, a chicken farmer, was car-jacked at gunpoint, beaten, and held for ransom for two days. He was released by his captors after his wife paid a ransom of EGP 300,000 ($43,200).

In January a group of hundreds of Muslim villagers tore down a Christian social center under construction in Ezbet Faouns village in Fayoum because it reportedly would be converted into a church, according to local press. According to EIPR, a villager used the village mosque's speakers to call on Muslims to "bring victory to Islam...the Christians are building a church." The police were reportedly informed of the incident but failed to protect the building. According to a local priest, police arrived after the building had been torn down, which took place over the course of approximately two hours, causing damage estimated at EGP 85,000 ($12, 300). Police failed to arrest any of the perpetrators.

The Morsy government failed to condemn or counter incendiary speech. Sectarian rhetoric was commonplace on Islamist satellite channels. Flyers were reportedly distributed by alleged Salafis among villagers in Beni Suef and Minya, threatening Christians with reprisals if they participated in the demonstrations scheduled for June 30. In their August 7 joint statement, non-governmental and civil society organizations strongly condemned the rhetoric employed by the Muslim Brotherhood leadership and their allies, which they characterized as "clear incitement to violence and religious hatred." Some Christian leaders saw violence against Copts as retaliation for their role in the June 30 demonstrations, which were widely viewed by many Islamists as orchestrated by the Coptic minority. Incendiary speech emanating from mosques was reportedly a factor in several instances of sectarian violence, such as the Abu Muslam lynching of four Shia, the Al Khosous incidents, and the attacks on churches August 14-17, according to reports prepared by EIPR, HRW, and the Arabic Network for Human Rights Information. Following the removal of former President Morsy, the interim government shut down 10 Islamist television channels for inciting violence, according to Egyptian satellite company Nilesat.

There were no indications in the media that the government enforced the 2011 amendments to the penal code that make discrimination a crime. The penal code defined discrimination as "any action, or lack of action, that leads to discrimination between people or against a sect due to gender, origin, language, religion, or belief." The new amendments established higher penalties for government officials than for other offenders.

Section III. Status of Societal Respect for Religious Freedom

There were reports of societal abuses and discrimination based on religious affiliation, belief, or practice. Lethal sectarian attacks increased during the year. Attacks on Christians, which had been on the rise since mass demonstrations against former President Morsy on June 30, spiked on August 14 after security forces forcibly cleared Muslim Brotherhood-led demonstrators from Raba'a El-Adawiya and Al Nahda Squares in Cairo, resulting in at least 600 deaths according to nongovernmental organizations. Islamist-led mobs carried out acts of violence, intimidation, compelled expulsions, and collective punishment against Christians, especially in Upper Egypt. NGOs reported assailants had attacked at least 42 churches in various governorates, but concentrated in Upper Egypt, in addition to

EGYPT

schools, orphanages, and other Christian-affiliated facilities between August 14 and August 17. The violence resulted in the looting and destruction of at least 37 churches and the deaths of at least six Christians who were targeted because of their religious identity. According to government officials, 194 suspects were arrested for attacks on churches and Christian-owned property on August 14 nationwide.

HRW reported crowds of men on trucks and on foot chanted anti-Christian slogans and threatened the Coptic community in Minya on August 14. The crowd looted the Al-Amir Tadros Coptic Church before setting the building on fire. An eyewitness account described the men around the church as armed with Molotov cocktails and at least five assault rifles. The crowd attacked and burned approximately 20 Christian-owned shops, three other churches, a Coptic boys' school complex, the Saint Joseph's Girls' School, the Gunud al-Maseeh Orphanage, and the Jesuit community center. Security forces were reportedly absent throughout these incidents, and emergency vehicles and firefighters did not come to extinguish the fires despite calls for help and the church being 20 meters from Minya governorate's security directorate. In similar attacks on the same day in Kerdasa, Giza, and Delga, police stations and churches were attacked simultaneously.

Reports indicate many attacks during this period followed a common pattern, with Islamists marching to churches or the homes of Christians and then looting and burning the property. Mob action also occurred during sectarian violence in the Fayoum Christian social center, the Abu Muslam lynching of Shia, and attacks in al-Dabaiya village in Luxor, Beni Ahmed village in Minya, and Al Wasta village in Beni Suef. In the aftermath of these attacks, communal tensions remained high, although Christians and Muslims shared a common culture and in most cases continued to live together peacefully in most areas of the country.

Anti-Shia rhetoric increased in the wake of a government initiative under former President Morsy to revive bilateral cooperation between Egypt and Iran. Following Morsy's meeting with then-Iranian President Mahmoud Ahmedinejad in Egypt in February, Grand Imam of Al Azhar, Ahmad El Tayyeb, issued a press release saying he "rejected the spread of Shi'ism" in Egypt, according to a report by HRW. Nevertheless, as part of the new cooperation between the two countries, a tourism exchange program was adopted. Prominent Salafi figures openly denounced the move, fearing it would lead to the spread of Shia Islam in Egypt. In April HRW reported that the Salafist Al-Nour Party organized a series of anti-Shia rallies under the banner of "Shia Are the Enemy, So Beware of Them" in

EGYPT

Alexandria, Kafr el Sheikh, and other cities. In May a member of parliament from the Al-Nour Party, Tharwat Attallah, reportedly stated that Shia "pose a danger to Egypt's national security," and called for an end to tourism from Iran, according to the same HRW report. Following months of opposition, mainly by Salafis, Tourism Minister Hisham Zazou announced in October that tourism links with Iran had been suspended for reasons of "national security," according to state television.

In August 4, two Sufi shrines were damaged by bomb attacks in the Sinai Peninsula. The shrines were in the towns of Bir el-Abd and el-Maghara. The General Sheikhdom of Sufi Ways accused Takfiri and Salafi jihadists of perpetrating the bombings.

There were reports of isolated but increasing land thefts from Christians, especially in Upper Egypt. In some cases informal "reconciliation sessions" were used to justify stealing or force the sale at low prices of small parcels of Christian-owned land. Some Christians reportedly decided to move from Muslim-majority villages to towns where they believed they would be more secure.

Certain media outlets published cartoons demonizing Jews and accusing them of seeking to subvert Egypt and Islam and take over the world. Private Salafi media sometimes included anti-Semitic programming that glorified or denied the Holocaust, including in interviews with academics and clerics. Privately owned Dream TV broadcast the anti-Semitic TV series "Khaiber" during Ramadan and "Horseman Without a Horse" in September, which included a story line around the Tsarist forgery, "The Protocols of the Elders of Zion." There were reports of imams using anti-Semitic rhetoric in their sermons, including allegations of blood libel.

Section IV. U.S. Government Policy

Officials at all levels of the U.S. government, including the President, Secretary and Deputy Secretary of State, Ambassador, Assistant Secretary for Democracy, Human Rights, and Labor, and other Department of State and embassy officials, raised religious freedom concerns with the government. These included cases in which the government did not protect religious minorities and their property or arrest and prosecute perpetrators of violence, as well as cases in which Christians received disproportionately severe sentences. Officials also raised the ongoing discrimination that Christians faced in building and maintaining church properties; official discrimination against Bahais; arrests and harassment of Muslim citizens whose religious views differed from the majority; anti-Semitism; and the government's treatment of Muslim citizens who wished to convert.

In August the President condemned sectarian violence in Egypt, including attacks on churches. In March and November the Secretary of State met with government officials and civil society leaders in Cairo. During his March visit, the Secretary emphasized the importance of ensuring freedom of religion for all Egyptians, regardless of their faith, with equal rights and protections under the law. During his November visit, the Secretary condemned violence against churches and worshipers and discussed with Foreign Minister Nabil Fahmy the need to hold perpetrators of such violence accountable. The Assistant Secretary of State for Democracy, Human Rights, and Labor delivered a public statement in Cairo in February in which he expressed U.S. support for the active political participation of all Egypt's citizens, including women, ethnic minorities, and Egyptians of all faiths.

The Ambassador made public statements supporting religious freedom, interfaith understanding, and efforts toward harmony and equality among members of all religious groups. In a March meeting with the Grand Mufti of Dar Al Iftah, the Ambassador recommended ways to reduce sectarian tensions and discrimination. Following the attack on St. Mark's Coptic Orthodox Cathedral in Abbasiya in April, the Ambassador raised religious freedom in meetings with the Prime Minister, top officials in the presidency, and the Minister of Justice. In May the Ambassador released a statement reaffirming the United States' position that freedom of religion is a universal right and encouraging the government to make improving the state of religious freedom in the country a top priority. In a June meeting with Pope Tawadros II, the Ambassador stressed U.S. support for defending universal human rights and religious freedom.

The embassy met regularly with officials in the Office of Human Rights at the Ministry of Foreign Affairs. The embassy also regularly discussed religious freedom matters with other government officials, including governors and members of parliament.

U.S. embassy officials maintained an active dialogue with leaders of the Jewish, Christian, Muslim, and Bahai religious communities, human rights groups, and other activists. U.S. embassy officials investigated complaints of official religious discrimination. They also discussed religious freedom matters with a range of contacts, including academics, business leaders, and citizens outside the capital area, including victims of sectarian violence in Upper Egypt. U.S. embassy

EGYPT

officials actively challenged anti-Semitic articles in the media through discussions with editors-in-chief and journalists.

The embassy supported the development of Arabic-language and English-language educational materials that encouraged tolerance, diversity, and understanding of others. The embassy also supported programs to promote tolerance among young religious leaders, interfaith understanding in communities that recently suffered from religious strife, and civic and political participation by marginalized youth. Embassy officials worked with the Supreme Council of Antiquities to promote the conservation of cultural antiquities, including Islamic, Christian, and Jewish historical sites.